Adam's Landing

Book 2

Zechariah Park

Adam's Landing

Cindy Holt Miller
Illustrated by Joe Eckstein

Four Fourteen
PUBLISHING

Indianapolis

Zechariah Park: Adam's Landing

Copyright © 2022 by Cindy Holt Miller. All rights reserved.
No portion of this book may be reproduced, stored in a retrieval system, or transmitted in any form or by any means, except for brief quotations in printed reviews, without prior permission of Cindy Holt Miller. Requests may be submitted by email at cindyholtmiller@gmail.com.

Illustrations Copyright © 2022 by Joe Eckstein
www.JoeEckstein.com

Published by Four Fourteen Publishing
Indianapolis, Indiana

Editing by Angie Zachery of Affordable Christian Editing

Cover and Interior Design by Imagine!® Studios
www.ArtsImagine.com

All Scripture quotations, unless otherwise indicated, are taken from The Holy Bible, New International Version® , NIV®. Copyright © 1973 1978 1984 2011 by Biblica, Inc.™ Used by permission. All rights reserved worldwide.

Scripture quotations marked MSG are taken from THE MESSAGE, copyright © 1993, 2002, 2018 by Eugene H. Peterson. Used by permission of NavPress, represented by Tyndale House Publishers. All rights reserved.

ISBN: 978-1-7371289-2-2
Library of Congress Control Number: 2022937053

First Four Fourteen Publishing printing: April 2022

For Kevin

Thank you for believing in me and my dreams. I loved singing and dancing through each day with you, loving Jesus, each other, our family and neighbors, just like Myrtle and Judah. You were truly a miracle from God for me. I will always love you.

Contents

Acknowledgements . . . . *viii*

Chapter 1
Adam's Landing 1

Chapter 2
Water into Wine 11

Chapter 3
Fishers of Men 24

Chapter 4
Calming the Storm 38

Chapter 5
Feeding Five Thousand 53

Chapter 6
Walking on Water 67

Chapter 7
The End of Summer Bash 80

Hide, Hide, Hide, I Hide Your Word in My Heart . . . *87*

About the Author & Illustrator *91*

Acknowledgements

My Heavenly Father, this is your book. May it accomplish all you want it to accomplish. "You are my God, and I will praise you; you are my God, and I will exalt you" (Psalm 118:28).

Kali, Mackenzie and Matt, thank you for your love and support. You are such blessings!

Joe Eckstein, I am grateful God brought us together. There is no one I would rather partner with to bring ZP to the world. You and your talents are a true gift. Thank you!

Angie Zachary, thank you for editing and proofreading *Adam's Landing*.

"Old men and old women will come back to Jerusalem, sit on benches on the streets and spin tales, move around safely with their canes—a good city to grow old in. And boys and girls will fill the public parks, laughing and playing— a good city to grow up in."

Zechariah 8:4–5 (MSG)

Chapter 1

Adam's Landing

Myrtle and Judah are excited about Zechariah Park's newest addition. Their grandson, Adam, moved to ZP and bought the yellow house at the north end of the neighborhood, next to a large lake. Adam turned the lake into a fun place for the ZP families to enjoy and named it **Adam's Landing at Zechariah Park**. It opens for the first time tomorrow. Today Adam is taking Myrtle and Judah, whom he calls Gran and Pops, on a tour of Adam's Landing.

Myrtle stood at her front door looking out at the cozy homes lining her street in beautiful Zechariah Park. She was excitedly waiting for Adam to arrive, with her bag, hat and sunglasses. Suddenly she heard a loud *quack, quack* and laughed as she called out, "Hurry, Judah! Adam is almost here in his duck boat."

Judah grabbed his cane and put on his hat as he replied, "Here I come. I wouldn't miss this for anything."

Adam pulled up in front of his grandparents' home in a funny-looking bright yellow vehicle with large orange lettering on the side that said *Adam's Landing at Zechariah Park*. It looked like a duck on wheels with a canopy on its back. Judah laughed when he saw it, and his heart swelled with pride. He loved his grandson.

Adam turned off the engine, walked to the back and put down the ramp so Myrtle and Judah could get in.

"Hey, Gran. Hey, Pops. I am excited for you to be the first riders in my new duck boat."

Adam kissed Myrtle on the cheek and reached for her hand. "Let me help you, Gran." Myrtle took his hand, and he walked her up the ramp to a seat at the front.

"Thanks, Sweetie! I am excited to see your Landing and ride in this crazy car/boat."

Judah was right behind them, laughing, "We are going to have AQGT."

Adam looked confused. "AQGT? What's that?"

At the same time, Myrtle and Judah said, "A Quacking Good Time."

"He has been saying that all morning," giggled Myrtle.

Adam laughed, "I can always count on you for the corny jokes, Pops. You quack me up." He gave Judah a high five as Myrtle said, "You are just like your Pops, Adam, only younger."

"And proud of it!" said Adam as he pulled up the ramp and walked to the front.

Adam sat down in the driver's seat, hit the start button, and the duck boat began moving through Zechariah Park, quacking. The neighbors laughed and waved as the duck boat passed, excited to see what Judah and Myrtle's grandson was bringing to the neighborhood.

Judah waved back and yelled, "Whoop, whoop, it's showtime! This is so much fun it makes me want to dance."

"Don't start dancing until we stop," cautioned Adam with a laugh that sounded just like his grandfather's.

As they pulled up in front of the Landing, Myrtle's eyes lit up. "Oh, this looks like such a fun place."

"Thanks, Gran. I hope the families of Zechariah Park have a lot of fun here."

"Do we get a tour?" asked Judah impatiently.

"Absolutely. We can get off the duck boat, walk into the marina and visit the observation deck on the roof to see everything, or we can stay in the duck boat and explore on both land and water sitting right here."

"Coolio. I want to explore by duck boat. My dear Myrtle, are you okay with that?" asked Judah.

Myrtle gave a thumbs up and said, "Duck boat tour it is."

"You two are the coolest grandparents around. Let's go!"

Adam blew the horn, and the quacks rang out as he turned the duck boat around and headed to the edge of the lake.

"Hold on to your hats! We are going into the water."

The duck boat bounced down the pier and splashed into the water. Before Myrtle and Judah knew what was happening, they were floating on the lake.

Judah took a deep breath and said, "Whoa, that was coolio! Do you think that's how ducks feel when they go from land to water?"

"Pops, you have made me laugh for as long as I can remember. Look over on the right, next to the clubhouse. That is the picnic area. Families can bring their picnic lunches or buy food from the Landing's snack bar."

As the duck boat floated past the picnic area, the beach came into view. Myrtle's eyes lit up as she exclaimed, "Judah, look!"

Adam smiled, "I had to make a special place for everyone's favorite ZP residents."

On the beach, a set of beach chairs sat under a big umbrella. The sign next to the chairs said *Reserved for Myrtle and Judah.*

"I know how much you love sitting on the beach, reading and watching people. So, this is a ZP version of your favorite beach. You can sit and watch the boats go by, the families swim, and your friends fishing and having fun with the kayaks and pedal boats. If you get hungry or thirsty, just call Zeke at the Landing. He will make sure you have what you need."

"What a sweetheart you are. Thank you!" beamed Myrtle with a smile.

Adam was happy Gran and Pops liked their special beach. "You are welcome! I am going to take you across the lake to see the marina, our rental boats and the cove. The trip across will take a few minutes, so relax and enjoy this beautiful lake."

As the duck boat floated across the water, Myrtle and Judah could see the buildings of the city off in the distance. The lake was calm, and the sun was glistening on the water. It did not seem long until the duck boat reached the marina where boats could be rented, and a sign read, *Book your fishing excursion here.*

"The ZP families are going to have so much fun on this lake. Can they take duck boat rides, too?" asked Judah.

"Yes. They can sign up at the clubhouse. Do you think people will enjoy riding on my duck boat?"

"No doubt! It is so unusual," replied Judah, shaking his head. "I never thought I could be riding down the street one minute and floating on water the next without changing vehicles."

"It's like a miracle," said Myrtle, giggling.

"Gran, that is what I want to share with the Zechariah Park kids this summer! The Bible tells us about the miracles Jesus performed when He lived on earth, and a lot of those involved water. It will be fun to help the ZP kids learn about Jesus' miracles involving water while having fun on the water at the same time.

"I want the Zechariah Park kids to realize that Jesus is God's Son. He is powerful enough to do miracles, yet He loves every one of them and wants them to love and follow Him, just like the disciples did."

"That makes your Gran excited," said Myrtle. "The ZP kids have to hear the stories in the Bible so they can hide God's Word in their hearts . . ."

"So, they know what to do when they don't know what to do," Adam and Judah piped up at the same time, finishing Myrtle's sentence.

"You have been telling me that since I was little," said Adam. "Now I want to share it with the ZP kids."

"I have a great idea!" exclaimed Judah.

"What's that?"

"I created a new version of my Tale Spinner. I call it the TSNN—Tale Spinner News Network. I program in Bible stories and this Tale Spinner creates an eyewitness account of the story that the ZP kids can see if they are wearing my Tale Spinner glasses. If you want to try it out, I will put in the stories about Jesus' miracles that we find in the Bible, and you can share them with our neighbors."

"That would be fun. Could you make two Tale Spinners? I could carry one with me and put one in the Landing so all of Zechariah Park can see these amazing things Jesus did."

"I will do that tonight before you open tomorrow," Judah agreed happily.

"Thanks! I have just the room in the Landing that would be perfect to show the Tale Spinner eyewitness accounts. We can call it the ZPH3 Theater, for Zechariah Park Hide, Hide, Hide," said Adam with a gleam in his eye.

"Yes! What a fun way for our Zechariah Park friends to hide God's Word in their hearts," exclaimed Myrtle as she patted her heart.

Raising his cane, Judah called out, "Let's sing it together!"

Hide, hide, hide, I hide your Word in my heart.
Hide, hide, hide, I hide your Word in my heart.

*So, I know what to do. So, I know what to do.
So, I know what to do, I won't sin against you.*'

Chapter 2

Water into Wine
(John 2:1–11)

> Do you know Jesus loves you so much he knows how many hairs are on your head? Matthew 10:29–31 tells us he does. If he loves you that much, don't you think he cares about everything that matters to you, including ice cream and having enough to drink at a wedding? Join Ava and Johnny as the Tale Spinner News Network shares with them about Jesus' first miracle. It was so incredible it convinced His new disciples that Jesus really was God's son.

"Congratulations on a successful opening day, Adam," said Mr. Williams as he and his family were enjoying ice cream at the Landing's snack bar with Myrtle, Judah, and Adam as the sun was setting over the lake.

"Thank you. After all that work and planning, it was fun to see our Zechariah Park friends have a great day," replied Adam, smiling.

Myrtle winked at Adam and said, "It was a good day, and the weather was perfect. I enjoyed sitting on our special beach chairs and watching the families have fun together. I am so proud of you."

"Thanks. I am happy all of you were here to share this day with me. Gran just told us her favorite part of the day; anyone else want to share their favorite part?"

Ava quickly swallowed her ice cream and said, "I had so much fun riding the pedal boat with Mom. My legs were really tired when we got off, but it was fun."

"I had fun pedaling across the lake with you, too," replied Mrs. Williams as she gave Ava a kiss on top of her head. "Thank you, Adam."

"My favorite part was the duck boat ride Johnny, and I took. I have never done anything like that," offered Mr. Williams. "As we drove down the ramp and bounced into the lake, I was sure we were going under water! But before I knew it, we were floating past the boats and seeing all the fun happening on the shore. Johnny was sure he saw fish in the lake as we floated across."

"I did! I wish I'd had a net; I could have reached out and caught some," giggled Johnny with a mischievous smile on this face.

Adam winked at Johnny and said, "You don't want to end up swimming with the fish, so your dad and I have to use a net to get you out of the lake."

"That would be fun to watch," giggled Ava.

Johnny stood up and said, "My friends and I had a blast at the beach. We swam, played frisbee and ate snacks. It was so much fun."

"My favorite part is this right here," said Judah as he held up his ice cream cone. "Ice cream is the coolest snack. Get it? Coolest? Ice cream is cold."

Everyone laughed as Judah pretended to dance in his chair.

Mr. Williams laughed. "Do you know what cats like on their birthday? Cake and mice cream."

"Oh, Dad," said Ava and Johnny at the same time.

"There is a secret about what happened with the ice cream. Do you want to hear about it?" asked Adam with a twinkle in his eye.

Judah narrowed his eyes and looked at his grandson. "Adam, are you keeping secrets from us? I thought I knew everything that was going on in Zechariah Park," he said as he playfully tapped his cane on the floor and then smiled.

"Please don't tell me this ice cream is made from fish!" said Johnny, a tad bit worried.

"It is nothing like that," assured Adam. "We had so many people come to our opening day that we almost ran out of ice cream."

Ava looked stunned and said, "That would have been a disaster. What happened?"

Adam sat back in his chair, adjusted his hat and began, "I was out on the speedboat with the new family that moved into Zechariah Park last weekend when my phone rang. It was Zeke from the snack bar. He was panicking because we were almost out of ice cream, and it was only the middle of the afternoon. I was shocked. We ordered what I thought was more than enough, but he told me twice as many people had come through the gates as we had planned for. I knew we needed to do something fast, but I was on a boat in the middle of the lake and not sure what to do.

"Suddenly, he stopped talking, then said, 'Hold on. I will call you back in just a minute.' I could not believe he hung up. I trusted him and kept driving the boat so our new family would have fun, but my stomach was in knots.

"Finally, my phone rang again. I picked it up, and Zeke was laughing. 'Adam, you are not going to believe this. As I was talking to you, the ice cream man came up to the window. He said he and his family visited this morning and had a fun time. There were so many people at the Landing, he knew we would need more ice cream. So, he loaded up his truck and said that he would like to give it to us as a thank you and to welcome Adam's Landing to Zechariah Park.'

"I could not believe what I was hearing. He brought the ice cream in, put it in the freezers and saved the day."

"Did that really happen or are you teasing us?" asked Ava suspiciously.

"It really happened," Adam assured her, shaking his head. "Can you believe it?"

"I believe it. God can and will do miracles for us if we invite Him into our lives. He cares about us and what we need. The Bible tells us in Philippians 4:19 that God will always supply our needs. That is exactly what He did for you today, Adam," said Myrtle as she patted her heart.

"He did it for all of us," exclaimed Johnny. "It would have been so sad to not have ice cream!"

Judah laughed as he agreed, "You are right, Johnny. Adam, do you remember when we prayed today before opening and asked God to bless the day and meet the needs of everyone who attended? He answered that prayer."

"You are so right, Pops . . ."

"Wait," said Ava, interrupting Adam. "Isn't there a story in the Bible about running out of something at a wedding and Jesus helped by performing a miracle?"

Adam winked at Judah and said, "There is. Should we try out the new Tale Spinner Pops made for me and watch what Jesus did? Johnny, will you run back behind the counter and grab the basket of Tale Spinner glasses? I will get the Tale Spinner from my office."

As Johnny ran behind the counter and brought the glasses to the table, Adam came back from his office and said, "We get to see Pops' newest invention, the Tale Spinner News Network and learn about Jesus' first public miracle. This miracle was so incredible it convinced His new disciples that Jesus really was God's Son. Do you all have on your Tale Spinner glasses?"

"Yes!"

Putting on his own Tale Spinner glasses, Adam laughed just like his grandfather and said, "I love this part!" He pushed the button on the pocket of his belt, and the Tale Spinner flew out. When Adam lifted it to his mouth and blew, out popped the Tale Spinner News Network.

"It's showtime. Here we go!" exclaimed Adam.

Hello, I am Mary, Jesus' mother. I want to share with you about my son's first public miracle. We were invited to the wedding celebration of our friends in Cana up in Galilee. Jesus and I, along with some of His new disciples, attended the wedding. At the party after the wedding, we were having a wonderful time, but I looked across the room and saw my friend, the mother of the groom, looking upset. I walked over to her and asked what was wrong. She quietly told me that so many people came to the wedding celebration, she was worried they were going to run out of wine.

In our day, weddings were important and lasted for days. It would have been embarrassing to invite people to a celebration and then run out of something for them to drink. I felt bad for her. My son, Jesus, cares about everyone, so I immediately thought He would be able to help. I found Him, told Him the wine was almost gone, and asked him to fix it.

Jesus looked at me and said, "That is none of our business, Mom. We should not get involved. It is not time for these people to know about Me yet."

Even though I am His mother, I knew I could trust Jesus to do what was best. I looked at the servants and asked them to do whatever Jesus told them to do. Then I went back to the celebration.

I am not sure what happened after I walked away, but before I knew it, the servants were putting clean water into the big empty jars that had been filled with water to wash the guests' hands. I walked over and asked one of the servants what he was doing. He said Jesus told them to fill the empty jars with water and then take a cup of the water to the man in charge of the party. The servant told me he was nervous to give this important man water from the jars used to wash the guests' hands.

Feeling sorry for him, I quietly told him, "Jesus can be trusted. Jesus may ask you to do what seems strange to you; but if you obey, you will be amazed at what He does." I patted him on the arm and walked back to the party.

It was not long until my friend, Hannah, came to me and said, "Mary, have you tried this?" as she held up a cup of wine. "It is the best I have ever tasted. You have to try some." I smiled as I agreed to try it. I looked back at where the servants were working. The servant I had encouraged to trust and obey Jesus smiled at me. I smiled back as John, one of Jesus' new disciples, walked by.

"John, what happened with the water?" I asked quietly. "Hannah told me it was the best wine she has ever tasted."

John looked astonished as he whispered, "Mary, it was amazing! Jesus told the servants to fill the pots with water and take a cup to the man in charge of the party. They did. He took one sip and looked surprised. He quickly walked over to the

groom and said, 'Everyone else I know serves the best tasting wine first. When the guests have had a lot to drink and are not as thirsty, then the cheaper wine is served. You saved the best for last!'

John shook his head and said, "Wow! I saw Jesus do this amazing miracle, Mary. He really is God's Son, isn't He?"

"Yes, He is," I responded.

Jesus had turned ordinary water into the best-tasting wine. This was just the first of many miracles I saw Jesus do in public.

Because His new disciples saw Jesus do this miracle, they realized Jesus was more than just the great teacher they had decided to follow. He was the Messiah, God's Son and the Savior of the world.

If Jesus cared enough to turn water into wine because the bride and groom needed it, he can help you, too. Ask Him; tell Him what you need. He loves and cares for you.

As their Tale Spinner glasses went dark, Adam said, "That's a wrap," and hit the retract button on his belt. The Tale Spinner spun around and flew back into his belt's secret compartment.

"I didn't know Jesus cared about the little things like having enough to drink at a wedding and making sure we don't run out of ice cream," said Johnny with wide eyes.

Looking at Johnny and Ava, Judah assured them, "Jesus loves you very much and cares about everything you care about, even the little things. Jesus tells us in Matthew 10:29–31 that God cares so much for the little birds that not one of them can fall to the ground without God knowing about it. Here is the cool part; He cares so much more for you, and He knows everything there is to know about you, including how many hairs you have on your head. If God loves you that much, don't you think He cares about everything that matters to you?"

"That is really amazing. Thank you for sharing that, Mr. Judah," said Ava. Then she patted her heart as she spoke again. "That is another good reason to hide God's Word in our hearts, so we always remember that."

"Oh, Sweet Ava. What you just said makes me want to dance like Judah," said Myrtle as she patted her own heart.

Adam started laughing. "I am sure it took God longer to count the hairs on my head than it did on yours, Pops." Everyone laughed as Judah pointed to his bald head.

Mrs. Williams looked at her watch and stood up, "It has been a long and exciting day, but it is time for this family to go home. Thank you, Adam, for bringing such fun to ZP. Kids, go throw away your trash so we can head home."

Judah stood up and reached for Myrtle's hand, "Let's walk home with our neighbors."

Myrtle put her arm through Judah's, then waved at Adam. As they walked out the door, Judah raised his cane and called out, "Let's sing it together!"

Hide, hide, hide, I hide your Word in my heart.
Hide, hide, hide, I hide your Word in my heart.
So, I know what to do. So, I know what to do.
So, I know what to do, I won't sin against you.

Chapter 3

Fishers of Men
(Luke 5:1–11)

Can you imagine catching so many fish you think your boat might sink? That is what happened to some fisherman when Jesus asked to borrow their boat. This miracle was so amazing, these fishermen decided to leave their boats, and their fishing business, to follow Jesus and become fishers of men. One of the fishermen, John, shares this story on the Tale Spinner News Network with some of the boys of ZP, and their dads, as they fish for breakfast.

Before the sun was even up, Carlos, Isaiah, Lucas and their dads walked through Zechariah Park towards the marina at Adam's Landing. They booked an early morning fishing excursion with Adam and were excited to see how many fish they could catch. As they walked up to the marina, they spotted Adam standing with Judah.

"Good morning, ZP friends! It is a beautiful morning to fish," declared Judah.

"Hi, Mr. Judah. Are you going fishing with us?" asked Isaiah.

"Not this morning," said Judah, "but my dear Myrtle and I will be waiting on the pier when you get back. We are going to clean and cook the fish you catch for breakfast."

"That sounds great! I know I will be hungry after a morning of fishing. Thank you," said Carlos' dad.

Adam patted his Pops on the shoulder and motioned for the others to get onto the boat. "If we don't get going, the sun will come up, and the fish will be harder to catch."

"Before you go, here is a fun fact," shared Judah with a twinkle in his eye. "Fish do not have eyelids, so the sunlight can bother them. That is why they go deeper in the water once the sun comes up."

"Is that really true, Mr. Judah?" asked Carlos.

"Have you ever seen a fish wink at you?" asked Judah as he winked at Carlos.

As everyone laughed, Adam said, "Pops could keep us laughing all morning, but we need to get going."

"I love fried fish, and you will too. So, go catch some fish and have fun," encouraged Judah as he pointed towards the boat.

Adam's boat had plenty of room to sit or stand while fishing and was well stocked with everything they would need. After everyone found a seat, Adam started the engine and the boat headed out through the darkness to the middle of the lake.

"How do you know where the fish are?" wondered Lucas aloud.

Adam pointed to a screen. "This handy, dandy contraption right here tells us."

As the boys and their dads crowded around what looked like a small computer screen, Adam continued. "It is called a fish finder and uses sound waves to locate objects in the water. If the sound waves detect something, it sends that information back to this screen. This lets us see how deep the fish are and where to cast our lines."

"That makes fishing a no-brainer," said Lucas' dad with a chuckle.

"As long as the fish are there, it is easy to catch them. My guess is Jesus' disciples, who were fisherman, wish they could have had a fish finder. Do you guys know the Bible story about Jesus showing some of His disciples where to fish?" asked Adam.

"No."

"I don't."

"Me, either"

"I have a good idea then. Pops invented the Tale Spinner News Network that tells us about some of the miracles Jesus did while living on Earth. Since we will have a better chance of catching more fish if we are not too loud right now, how about we watch the Tale Spinner account of Jesus helping His disciples fish while Gran and Pops cook breakfast once we're back."

"Sounds good to me," said Carlos.

"Alright. Here we go."

As the boat pushed through the water, the lake was quiet. The birds were singing from the trees on the shore as city lights began coming on in the distance.

The sound of the motor stopped. Adam turned around and said, "This is the spot. We have a school of fish under the boat looking for breakfast, so this might be easy. Let's catch some fish!" explained Adam, excited about the possibility of pulling in a lot of fish at one time.

Once the bait was on the lines, the dads and Adam helped the boys cast them into the water.

"Don't let go of the pole," cautioned Adam. "According to the fish finder, there are some big fish down there."

"I got one!" yelled Lucas.

As they tried to pull in the fish, it wiggled off the hook and swam away.

"Oh no, I lost him!"

Adam patted Lucas on the shoulder. "Don't be discouraged. Get another worm and try again."

"Oh," yelled Isaiah excitedly. "Something is pulling on my line. Is it a fish?"

"Probably, the fish finder says a whole lot of fish are underneath our boat swimming towards your worms," Adam replied happily.

"Let me help you, son," said Isaiah's dad as he showed Isaiah how to reel in the fish.

"Pull him in. We will take out the hook and put him on ice to keep him fresh until we can get him to Pops," instructed Adam.

Before long, Carlos and his dad both caught a fish. As soon as both fish were on ice in the cooler, Lucas yelled, "I have another one! Help me, I don't want to lose him again."

Lucas' dad and Adam helped reel in the fish. Lucas was so excited he was jumping for joy as his dad took the fish off the hook.

It seemed the fish were hungry, so Adam was busy running back and forth helping the boys and their dads reel in the fish. By the time the sun was completely up, they had caught enough fish for breakfast and leftovers. It was time to go back to the marina. Adam called Pops and told him to head to the pier to pick up the catch.

On the ride back everyone was trying to decide who caught the biggest fish.

"I don't care who caught the biggest fish, as long as I get to eat. I am starving," declared Isaiah.

Adam laughed and agreed, "Me, too. Look, Gran and Pops are waiting on the pier for our fish. I hope Gran is making scrambled eggs and her famous blueberry muffins."

Adam steered the boat up to the pier and threw out the ropes. Judah secured the boat as the dads carried the coolers to Judah's wagon.

"Can I help you pull this into the marina?" asked Lucas' dad.

"Thank you, my friend, but I can do it. I will let you go back to the boat and help the boys hide more of God's Word in their hearts by seeing how Jesus helped His disciples catch a boat load of fish. My dear Myrtle and I will have a good breakfast waiting for you when you are done," Judah assured him.

As Lucas' dad walked back onto the boat, he saw Adam passing out Tale Spinner glasses as everyone found a comfortable place to sit.

"If you are ready to hear about Jesus' miracle that was so incredible some fishermen decided to leave their boats and their fishing business to become His disciples, then put on those glasses," said Adam with a chuckle.

While putting on his own Tale Spinner glasses, Adam laughed just like his grandfather and said, "I love this part!" He pushed the button on the pocket of his belt, and the Tale Spinner flew out. When Adam lifted it to his mouth and blew, out popped the Tale Spinner News Network.

"It's showtime. Here we go!" exclaimed Adam.

My name is John, and I want to share with you how I became a fisher of men. That sounds strange, but I promise, it is an amazing story.

Let me first tell you about my life before I met Jesus. My family and I lived in a town on the edge of the Sea of Galilee. My brother, James, and I, along with our friends, Simon Peter and Andrew, owned a fishing business. Each evening, we would take our boats out into the water to fish. Early each morning, we sailed back to shore and sold the fish we had caught to the people in our city. That was how we provided for our families.

We usually caught a lot of fish, but one night, things were different. We had been fishing in two different boats all night long and caught no fish at all. We were tired and discouraged. The sun was coming up, and we knew it was time to head back to shore. You see, when the sun comes out, the fish dive down into deeper waters where it is cool, and it is more difficult to catch them. Plus, we used nets to catch fish and when the sun was out, it seemed the fish could see our nets and stayed away from them. The fish in the Sea of Galilee were smart and knew what to do to keep from landing in our nets.

We headed back to the shore and began washing the nets so they would be ready for the next morning. As we worked, we noticed a crowd of people near the edge of the water listening to a man called Jesus. Everyone in our city had been talking about this great teacher. We even heard about Him healing people everywhere He went. I wanted to listen to Jesus, but I was tired. I really needed to just wash my nets and go home to sleep.

The crowd was so large, Jesus needed more space. He saw our empty boats sitting at the edge of the lake and walked over to us. Jesus asked my business partner, Simon, if He could use his boat. Simon, who later was called Peter, heard about Jesus from the people buying his fish each morning. He was curious so he said yes. Simon pushed the boat out into the water, jumped into the boat with Jesus and took Him out a little way from the shore. Being on the water helped His voice carry to the crowd, so Jesus sat in the boat teaching the people on the shore for a long time. We sat down and listened. Jesus, the man everyone had been talking about, was using one of our boats. Our dad, Zebedee, thought that was awesome.

Jesus finished teaching, looked at Simon and said, "Let's go fishing. Take the boat out farther and throw out your nets."

Simon told us later he thought that was not a good idea because we had just spent the entire night fishing and caught no fish. But Jesus was a great teacher, and Simon wanted to be respectful, so he agreed. They turned the boat around and headed into deeper water. When they reached the middle of the lake, in the exact spot where we had spent the night fishing, Jesus told Simon to throw the nets into the water.

Simon replied, "We have been fishing in this area all night and have caught nothing, but if You tell me to throw out my nets, I'll do it."

Simon threw out the nets and immediately began yelling for my brother and me to bring the other boat out quickly. We jumped in our boat and headed out to help Simon. So many fish were in the

nets, they were about to break. We could not believe what we were seeing.

We threw our nets out and they were immediately filled with fish, too. Seeing all those fish was unbelievable. We caught so many fish I thought our boats might sink. We knew then that Jesus was more than just a good teacher, and all four of us wanted to learn more; but to be honest, we were a little frightened.

When we got back to shore, Jesus knew we were frightened and said, "Don't be afraid. Come and follow Me. Help Me tell others that God loves them and, instead of being fishermen, you can become fishers of men."

We decided right then we would give up everything and follow Jesus. We left our boats, filled with fish, on the shore and became His disciples. That day, I went from catching fish to being a fisher of men.

We knew Jesus did not mean we would catch people in our nets like we caught fish. He meant that if we followed Him and became His disciples, we could tell others about Him and, hopefully, they would also begin following Jesus.

Deciding to follow Jesus was the best decision I ever made! I hope you will follow Jesus, too. Just as Jesus called my friends and me to follow Him and *become fishers of men, He is calling you to become fishers of your friends and neighbors. Will you tell your friends about Jesus and let them know how much He loves them?*

As their Tale Spinner glasses went dark, Adam said, "That's a wrap," and hit the retract button on his belt. The Tale Spinner spun around and flew back into his belt's secret compartment.

Lucas' dad said, "That was incredible. I think it would have been awesome to be able to follow Jesus around when He was on Earth and see Him do all of these miracles that only He could do."

"I would have liked that, too," agreed Lucas. "Isaiah showed me that we can be followers of Jesus and do the right thing even on the playground. Do you guys remember when that happened?"

Carlos gave his friend a fist bump and said, "I do remember. It was my first day of school, and Isaiah asked me to play basketball at recess with you. I was shy, but I said yes. You showed the love of Jesus to me, and now we have become good friends. I am glad we are all followers of Jesus."

Isaiah's dad winked at him as Isaiah said, "It is not always easy to be a follower of Jesus, but it is important to always do the right thing."

"Can you imagine if we had caught as many fish this morning as Jesus helped the disciples catch?" asked Lucas with big eyes.

Carlos laughed. "We would never be able to eat that many fish for breakfast."

"Probably not, but I am ready to eat the fish we did catch. I'm really hungry now," declared Isaiah, rubbing his stomach.

"It smells like Gran and Pops have our breakfast ready. Let's go eat," invited Adam as he stood up. "Don't forget to drop your Tale Spinner glasses in the basket before getting off the boat."

As the boys and their dads began following Adam down the pier and into the Landing's marina for breakfast, you could hear them whistling Judah's favorite song:

Hide, hide, hide, I hide your Word in my heart.
Hide, hide, hide, I hide your Word in my heart.
So, I know what to do. So, I know what to do.
So, I know what to do, I won't sin against you.

Chapter 4

Calming the Storm
(Mark 4:35–41)

> Have you ever been frightened? Rosie was riding on Adam's duck boat during a storm, and she was scared. She had hidden Psalm 56:3 in her heart and knew God would keep her safe. One of Jesus' disciples, James, was frightened when he was on a boat with Jesus during a storm, too. Join Rosie, Grace and their cousins as they put on their Tale Spinner glasses and watch James talk about the miracle Jesus did during the storm that made him believe Jesus really was God's son.

"Are you ready?" asked Mr. Harrison as he headed to the garage.

"Almost," answered Mrs. Harrison as she finished putting Grace's hair in a ponytail.

Rosie grabbed her beach bag and exclaimed, "I'm so excited!" as she ran out to the garage.

"Please hurry, Mama, I don't want them to leave without us," urged Grace impatiently.

"Done," said Mrs. Harrison as she finished securing Grace's ponytail. "Grab your beach bag; I'll grab the picnic basket and meet you in the garage."

The Harrisons, along with Uncle Mac, Aunt Joni, and their cousins, Evie and Isaac, who lived on the other side of Zechariah Park, were going to have a spectacular day playing in the bumper boats in the shallow waters of the cove.

As the Harrisons approached the Landing, Isaac caught a glimpse of his cousins and yelled, "There they are!"

When Adam saw them, he blew his duck whistle and asked, "Are you ready for a quacking good time? Let's go!"

Adam led the way to the bright yellow and orange duck boat. The ZP families climbed aboard and found their seats. Adam turned on the engine, blew the horn and the quacks rang out as the duck boat headed to the edge of the lake.

Isaac nervously asked Adam, "Is this really going to drive on the bottom of the lake? Will the water be over our heads?"

"When this duck boat hits the water, it floats and becomes a boat instead of a bus, so you don't have to worry about going under," assured Adam.

Giggling, Rosie added, "I bet Mr. Judah would say that is coolio."

"You know he would. Hold on, here we go," said Adam as the duck boat bounced down the ramp and into the lake.

The lake was smooth, and the sun was shining as they floated across the water.

"What a perfect day for bumper boats," Uncle Mac said with a smile.

Adam pointed to a group of trees just ahead that looked like a doorway. "That is the entrance to the cove. It is narrow and too shallow for boats to fit through, so thank goodness we have this crazy car/boat that works on land and water. Hold on, here we go!"

Adam drove onto the shore, through the trees, and into the shallow waters of the cove.

"Whoa, look at all those bumper boats!" said Isaac as the other side of the cove came into view.

Adam steered the duck boat through the shallow waters and parked on the shore behind the picnic tables.

"We have four hours to play, and then we will head back across the lake. It looks like the weather is going to cooperate, so let's have fun."

Adam walked to the back of the boat and lowered the ramp. The kids headed to the beach chairs while Mrs. Harrison and Aunt Joni put the picnic baskets on the picnic tables. It did not take long for everyone to choose their boats and push them into the water. Mr. Harrison and Uncle Mac were laughing as their boats bumped into each other. Rosie, Evie and Aunt Joni were trying to stay away from Isaac and Grace who were chasing them in their boats. Mrs. Harrison was enjoying the scene from a beach chair at the edge of the water.

Adam was sitting at a picnic table working on his computer when his phone buzzed. It was a text from his Gran, Myrtle. He read it, sighed, then clicked on the weather app. A sudden summer storm was developing. A thunderstorm warning and wind advisory had just been issued. Hearing the laughter and seeing the fun his friends were having, made Adam's heart sink. He knew it would take a while to get back across the lake in the duck boat. If they waited too long, the water could be choppy and dangerous. He looked at the sky again; there was no sign of a storm.

Adam picked up his phone. "Hey, Gran, thanks for the heads up on the storm."

"Hi, Sweetie. Radar is showing that the storm will be moving into our area in the next half hour. It is a fast-moving storm with heavy rain, strong winds, thunder and lightning. I don't want you and our friends to get stuck at the cove," said his grandmother.

"I know, but there is not a cloud in the sky. I wonder if I can wait a little longer."

"Just remember the weather can change quickly, Sweetie. I will pray you know what to do. Love you!"

"Love you, too, Gran."

Adam looked at the water, then up at the sky; it was clear and beautiful. Did he have time to let the Harrisons and their family play a little longer? He did not know what to do. Adam whispered a prayer and asked God to give him wisdom.

As he sat at the table wondering what to do, he suddenly felt it was time to go. Adam turned off his computer and ran to the edge of the lake. He yelled as he ran into the water, "A fast-moving summer storm is coming in. We need to get everyone out of the water, now."

Mrs. Harrison and Aunt Joni jumped up from their beach chairs and ran into the water to help bring the boats back in.

Mr. Harrison looked up and pointed to the western sky. "We need to hurry. The sky is already getting dark."

The kids jumped on the duck boat as the parents and Adam loaded the lunches and bags. Adam pulled up the ramp, ran to the front and turned on the engine. "Hold on! Let's get across the lake quickly." He drove the boat across the shallow water of the cove, back on land, through the trees and onto the big lake.

"That was a bumpy ride," said Evie. "I didn't like it."

Aunt Joni gave her daughter a reassuring hug.

The wind was picking up, and the sky was getting darker. Adam was pushing the duck boat as fast as it would go. Suddenly a streak of lightning flashed across the sky, followed by a loud clap of thunder.

"Hold on, we are almost there," Adam called out.

Rosie patted her heart as it began to rain. She kept repeating to herself, "When I am afraid, I put my trust

in you." She was thankful she had hidden this verse from the Bible in her heart a long time ago.

"Mr. Harrison, as soon as I stop, will you let down the ramp?" asked Adam as he pulled onto the shore.

He pulled up to the door and turned off the motor so his ZP friends could run into the Landing.

"Whew, we made it," exclaimed Grace. "I was really scared."

"I was a little scared, too," said Adam. "Aren't we glad God kept us safe?"

"That is just like the song I made up from a Bible verse I have hidden in my heart. Want to hear it?"

"Yes, sing it Grace."

Grace smiled, tilted her head and began singing:

"We trust in God. We trust in God,
And he will keep us safe when we are afraid.

I sing it when I am afraid to go to sleep, but I thought it was a good verse for the duck boat, too."

"Yay, Grace! I like that song. As Pops would say, coolio!

Is anyone else hungry? If so, I have a great idea. We can bring our picnic into the ZPH3 Theater and eat while we watch a Tale Spinner News Network broadcast. One story in the Bible talks about Jesus sleeping on a boat during a storm, and His disciples were frightened. This story even mentions Jesus' cousin, John. Would you cousins like to see it?"

"Yes."

"Okay, you get started on your lunch, and I will be right there."

After parking the duck boat, Adam walked into the theater and passed around a basket of Tale Spinner glasses. "You'll need these glasses to see the story."

While putting on his own Tale Spinner glasses, Adam's laugh sounded just like his grandfather's as he announced, "I love this part!" He pushed the button on the pocket of his belt, and the Tale Spinner flew out. When Adam lifted it to his mouth and blew, out popped the Tale Spinner News Network.

"It's showtime. Here we go!" exclaimed Adam.

My name is James; I am one of Jesus' disciples. I saw Him perform many miracles, but I want to tell you about the one that made me believe Jesus really was God's Son. Before I share that story, let me tell you what happened before the miracle to help you understand.

Just before Jesus began traveling and teaching, a man named John the Baptist came on the scene. John wore clothing made from camel's hair and a leather belt, and he ate locusts and wild honey. He was an unusual guy, and people walked miles to see and hear him.

By the way, John's dad's name was Zechariah, the same as your neighborhood. John's mother was Elizabeth, and she was a cousin to Jesus' mother, Mary. That means John was Jesus' cousin.

John the Baptist said he was just a messenger and that someone was coming after him who was so great John could not even be His servant. He told the people this man would change their lives if they would turn their back on sin so God could forgive them. John was talking about Jesus.

John baptized the people who came to listen to him in the Jordan River as a sign to the world that they had repented of their sins, decided to stop doing wrong, and live for God.

Before Jesus began traveling around and teaching, he went to the Jordan River and asked John to baptize Him. As Jesus came up out of the water, the sky opened, and the Holy Spirit, looking like a dove, appeared above Jesus' head. Then, a loud booming voice from Heaven said, "This is My Son. I love Him very much and am proud of him!"

That got everyone's attention. People began wondering and asking each other if Jesus could really be God's Son. They all wanted to see this Jesus with their own eyes, so crowds began going to wherever Jesus was to see and listen to Him.

This is where my story begins. My brother John and I and some of our friends decided to become followers of Jesus, and we traveled with Him. We were called His disciples. One day, Jesus was preaching beside the sea, and a large crowd gathered to listen. The people were pushing in to get close to Jesus until there was no more room on the shore. We found a boat so Jesus could sit in it out on the water and teach the people.

At the end of the day, Jesus was tired. He wanted to go to the other side of the lake to rest. We left the crowds on the shore and headed across the water. Jesus was exhausted, so He went to the back of the boat, found a cushion and fell asleep.

Calming the Storm

As we reached the middle of the lake, the sky was dark, and the wind was blowing furiously. Jesus was sleeping. It began to rain, thunder crashed, and lightning flashed across the sky. The boat was rocking back and forth so much that we were afraid it might flip over, but Jesus kept on sleeping. We wondered why he did not wake up. Did He not care about our safety?

We screamed, "Teacher, don't You care if we drown?"

Jesus rubbed His eyes and got up. He looked out at the waves as the thunder roared and lightning crashed and said, "Quiet, be still!"

Immediately, the wind, the waves, the thunder, the lightning . . . it all just stopped. We looked at each other, hardly believing what we had just witnessed. Jesus did this!

We had seen Him do miracles before. We watched as He healed Simon's mother-in-law, a man with leprosy, and another man in Capernaum who was paralyzed; but we were still amazed. We knew Jesus was special, but this stunned us. Even the wind and the waves obeyed Jesus.

He looked at us after telling the storm to stop and asked, "Why were you afraid? Where is your faith?"

We did not know what to say. We knew Jesus was more than just a great teacher; that is why we became His disciples. But seeing the wind and waves obey Him made us realize that He must really be the Son of God. I will never forget that day! It was the day I knew without a doubt that Jesus was God's Son. I hope you believe it, too!

As their Tale Spinner glasses went dark, Adam called out, "That's a wrap," as he hit the retract button on his belt. The Tale Spinner spun around and flew back into his belt's secret compartment.

"I think their boat ride was scarier than our duck boat ride," said Evie.

"Me, too," said Isaac. "I was so scared; I was praying the whole time. The disciples must have been really scared."

Mrs. Harrison smiled at her nephew and said, "Isaac, aren't you happy Jesus answered your prayer and kept us safe, just like He kept the disciples safe?"

"I know I am glad," said Uncle Mac. He then looked at Rosie and asked, "Why were you patting your heart the whole time?".

Rosie smiled and patted her heart again. "I was scared, but I remember when Mom taught me the Bible verse that says, 'When I am afraid, I put my trust in you.' I hid that verse in my heart, and patting my heart just reminds me of it."

"That would make Gran so proud to hear you say that, Rosie. She always tells us how important it is to hide God's Word in our hearts," said Adam as he gave Rosie a fist bump.

Mr. Harrison stood up, "This day did not turn out like we thought, but it has been a good day. Thanks, Adam. We will try it again another day. It's time to go home now."

"Do you know what Mr. Judah and Miss Myrtle would do if they were here now?" asked Evie.

Grace pretended to raise a cane in the air and called out, "Let's sing and dance all the way home."

The families laughed, waved goodbye to each other and headed down the sidewalk towards their homes singing:

Hide, hide, hide, I hide your Word in my heart.
Hide, hide, hide, I hide your Word in my heart.
So, I know what to do. So, I know what to do.
So, I know what to do, I won't sin against you.

Chapter 5

Feeding Five Thousand
(John 6:1–15)

Do you know God can use you, no matter how old you are? Jesus used a little boy's lunch to feed over five thousand hungry people and there were leftovers. Sounds unbelievable but the Bible tells us it really happened. Join Miles, Nori and Maria as they hear Andrew, one of Jesus' disciples, and Ben, whose lunch Jesus used, talk about this amazing miracle Jesus performed on the Tale Spinner News Network. Ben gave his little lunch to Jesus and Jesus did a big miracle with it.

"Thanks, Mom. That was a great lunch," said Maria after a picnic at the Landing with Miles, Nori, her mom and grandma.

"You are welcome, Sweet Maria. You needed a good lunch after a fun morning of swimming."

Maria's grandmother pushed up her sunglasses and said with a chuckle, "Swimming was fun, but it is so hot sitting here in the sun, I think the chocolate chips in my cookies are close to melting."

"Oh, no! We can't let the chocolate chips melt. I need to be able to bite into them when I eat your cookies," said Miles as he grabbed another one of Maria's grandmother's famous chocolate chip cookies. Miles looked at Maria's grandmother, the container of cookies and then asked, "Can I call you Grandma?"

Maria's grandmother laughed as she replied, "Yes, I would like that."

"If I do, will you make as many cookies for me as you do for Maria? You make the best chocolate chip cookies in the world, Grandma," said Miles with a smile.

"You are so funny, Miles," said Maria. "Nori, is she going to be your grandmother, too?"

"Maybe," said Nori as she took another bite of her cookie and asked, "Can I call you Grandma Cookie?"

The friends laughed as Grandma replied, "I will be Grandma Cookie if I can call you my little cookie."

Maria's mom laughed and asked, "Do you know why the chocolate chip cookie went to the doctor? Because he felt crummy."

"Oh, that's a good one," giggled Maria as her friends chuckled.

Just then, Judah walked by. "It looks like this table is having fun. Myrtle and I are sitting on our chairs under the umbrella and heard you laughing all the way down by the lake."

"Grandma has agreed to let Miles and Nori call her Grandma Cookie if she can call them her little cookies. Isn't that funny, Mr. Judah?" asked Maria, giggling.

"That is funny," Judah agreed, winking at Grandma. "Is that because Grandma makes the best chocolate chip cookies in Zechariah Park?"

Grandma picked up the container and offered a cookie to Judah. "Would you like one?"

"No, Myrtle has me on a diet, but thank you anyway."

"Mr. Judah, you have to call her Grandma Cookie, too," urged Nori.

"Wait," interrupted Miles, "If everyone calls her Grandma Cookie, she has to make cookies for everyone; and then we would have to share. I don't want to share my cookies."

"You can't eat all the cookies, Miles," said Grandma, shaking her head. "You will get sick."

"Plus, that's not nice," reminded Maria.

"It's just cookies. We don't have enough to feed all of Zechariah Park anyway."

Maria's mom looked at Judah and said, "That reminds me of a story about the boy who shared his little lunch with Jesus and something big happened. Would you share that story, Mr. Judah?"

Judah put his hand on his chin and said, "Hmm, I think that might be a good idea. Are you interested, Miles? I will call Adam and see if I can borrow his Tale Spinner for the News Network. Myrtle has some extra Tale Spinner glasses in her bag."

Miles shrugged and said, "Sure, why not."

"I want to see it," Maria squealed excitedly.

"Me, too," agreed Nori.

"Ok," said Judah as he reached into his pocket, for his phone.

Suddenly, they heard Adam's voice talking to other people on the beach.

Judah looked up. "Well, what do you know? Adam's here. Let's see if he has the Tale Spinner with him."

Adam saw his Pops and walked over to the group. "Hey, guys. It looks like you have been swimming and had a picnic."

Judah gave Adam a fist bump and shared, "Maria's grandma makes the best chocolate chip cookies in Zechariah Park, and the kids are now calling her Grandma Cookie."

"Grandma Cookie, I like that," said Adam.

Judah looked at his grandson and asked, "Do you have the Tale Spinner for the News Network with you? The kids would like to see what happened when a little boy shared his lunch with Jesus."

Adam patted his belt as he answered, "It is right here in the secret compartment you built. I don't have any Tale Spinner glasses with me though."

"That's ok, Gran has extras in her bag," replied Judah. "Should we all go down and sit under the umbrella with Myrtle and listen to one of Jesus' disciples tell us about this amazing miracle?"

"Let's go," said Miles.

Adam pushed the button on the pocket of his belt, and the Tale Spinner flew out. He gave it to Judah as everyone ran down the beach to sit under the giant umbrella with Myrtle.

"Hi, Miss Myrtle. Can we watch a Tale Spinner News Network story with you? Mr. Judah said it would be okay," asked Maria.

"Of course! Squeeze in under the umbrella while I get some Tale Spinner glasses for you," offered Myrtle, happy to have her friends join her. Myrtle opened her bag and passed out the glasses as Judah sat down in his chair and asked, "Do you all have on your glasses?"

"We do!"

While putting on his own Tale Spinner glasses, Judah laughed and said, "I love this part!" When he lifted the Tale Spinner to his mouth and blew, out popped the Tale Spinner News Network.

"It's showtime. Here we go!" exclaimed Judah.

"Hi, Zechariah Park. My name is Andrew, and I am a disciple of Jesus. This is my friend, Ben. We are going to take turns telling you about something spectacular that really happened to us when Jesus was living on Earth. Jesus performed miracles, healed sick people and told stories He called parables to teach lessons. He became famous, and crowds followed him everywhere.

One day, after spending time teaching and talking with people, Jesus heard that His cousin, John the Baptist, had been killed. He wanted to be by Himself for a while, so we found a boat and sailed with Him to what we thought was going to be a quiet place. But as we came close to the shore, we saw a lot of people gathered at the edge of the lake. I asked Jesus if He wanted me to find a quieter place. He looked at the crowd waiting for Him and said no.

Even though Jesus was sad and tired, He loved the people in the crowd. They had waited for Him, and He would not disappoint them. Jesus got out of the boat and found a large rock on the edge of the lake. He sat down and began talking with the people, healing the sick and telling His stories. He was such a great teacher that people listened for hours.

Later in the afternoon, we began to hear that the people were getting hungry. We went to Jesus and asked Him to tell the crowd to go home and get something to eat.

Jesus told us we should feed the people.

We could not believe what Jesus said. We did not have food for this crowd and were not sure what to do. That is where Ben comes in. I'll let Ben tell you what happened next."

Ben cleared his throat and began, "Well, my neighbor was telling everyone that Jesus was coming to our town. I wanted my mom to take me to see Him, but she had to stay at home with my little brother and sister. I really wanted to go hear Jesus, so I talked her into letting me go by myself. Mom packed five little loaves of bread and two fish in a basket and made me promise I would eat it for lunch. I promised, gave her a hug and ran out the door.

I saw many people down by the lake, so I started running. I was excited to see and hear Jesus in person. I found a rock, climbed on top of it and began listening to Jesus talk. I could understand everything He was saying.

In the middle of the afternoon, Andrew walked by. He saw my basket sitting on the rock and asked what was in it. I told him my mom made me lunch, but I had been too busy listening to Jesus to eat it. He smiled and agreed that listening to Jesus was amazing.

Andrew walked on, and I went back to watching Jesus heal people and share stories.

Later, Andrew came back and asked if I had eaten my lunch.

I said no. So, he told me Jesus wanted to see me, and my lunch.

Wow! Jesus wanted to see me! I grabbed my basket and followed Andrew. As we were walking toward Jesus, the other disciples were telling the people to sit down in groups. I was so excited I had butterflies in my stomach.

Andrew introduced me to Jesus, and Jesus asked if He could have my lunch. I was hungry, but I gave it to Jesus. He raised it up to Heaven and thanked God for it. Then He tore the bread in half and began giving bread and fish to the disciples to pass out to the people. I could not believe what I was seeing. The more the disciples shared my lunch, the more food there was. Before long, all those people

had eaten from my five loaves of bread and two fish. Wow! I could not wait to tell my mom."

Andrew shook his head and said, "Wow is right! And here is another wow. After everyone had eaten all they wanted, Jesus told us to pick up the leftovers. We gathered twelve baskets of bread and fish. Twelve! Jesus took Ben's lunch, fed 5,000 men plus their wives and children, and there were twelve baskets left over."

Andrew looked at Ben and said, "Tell them what your mom did when you told her what happened."

Ben smiled and began, "As I was telling Mom about the day, our neighbor knocked on the door. She had been there listening to Jesus and could not wait to tell Mom what Jesus did with my lunch, the lunch she made for me. My mom could not believe it. That very day, she decided to follow Jesus, too."

Andrew patted Ben on the shoulder and said, "That is why Jesus performed these miracles. After He used Ben's lunch to feed the crowd, many people repented of their sins and decided to become followers of Jesus. As word spread of another miracle, even more people began to realize Jesus could do anything, and He truly was the Son of God.

> *Ben agreed to give his lunch to Jesus and Jesus did something amazing with it. Never forget that God can take the little we have and use it greatly if we will let Him."*

Just as the Tale Spinner glasses went dark, Adam walked up next to Judah and pressed the retract button on his belt. The Tale Spinner spun around and flew back into his belt's secret compartment as Judah declared, "That's a wrap."

"That was awesome. I would share the cookies Grandma made for me with Jesus if I could," said Miles.

Myrtle smiled at Miles and said, "You know what, Miles? I bet you could figure out a way to share something like cookies with Jesus, and He would use them."

"Huh? What do you mean, Miss Myrtle? How could I share cookies with Jesus to use?" asked Miles with a confused look on his face.

Grandma patted Miles on the arm as she spoke. "Miss Myrtle is telling you that Jesus uses people to help people. What do you have, other than cookies, which could help someone else?"

Maria asked, "Are you asking what we could do for our friends and family that would make Jesus happy?"

Myrtle smiled. "That's it, Maria. Colossians 3:17 tells us that whatever we do, whether it is words or actions, should be said or done for Jesus. That is another good verse to hide in your heart to help you remember this," said Myrtle as she patted her heart.

Miles scratched his head and said, "Last week, we were playing baseball in the park when Johnny missed catching the ball at home plate. Isaiah made a home run, and our team lost the game. Johnny felt bad, and I was a little mad at him. Then I remembered the Bible verse I hid in my heart that says we should always be kind and forgive each other. I told him it was okay and that we all make mistakes. Is that what you mean?"

"That's it, Miles," said Judah excitedly. "That verse in Ephesians 4:32 reminded you to be kind and forgive Johnny. Jesus used your words to help Johnny just like he used Ben's lunch to help feed the crowd."

Myrtle patted her heart and said, "That is why it is important to hide God's Word in your heart. It helped you know the right thing to do to help Johnny. Yay, Miles!"

Looking puzzled, Nori asked. "But Mr. Judah, couldn't Jesus have made enough food for everyone without Ben's lunch?"

"Yes, Nori, He could have. Jesus didn't need Ben's lunch to feed the crowd, but He wanted Ben to see that God could use him, even though he was just a little boy."

"You know," began Adam, "I believe Jesus wanted the disciples, and the other people in the crowd, to see that He can use something very small to do something very big. Just like Andrew said on the Tale Spinner News Network, "God can take the little we have and use it greatly if we will let Him. My guess is that Jesus would be happy if you all would remember that every day. Nothing is too small to matter to God or too small for Him to use if you give it to Him."

"Grandma Cookie," said Nori with a giggle, "I think you should make fish and bread cookies to help us remember how Ben gave his little lunch to Jesus and Jesus did a big miracle with it."

"Yuck!" yelled Miles.

Grandma laughed as Maria said, "Stick with chocolate chip cookies, Grandma. We'll work on hiding God's Word in our hearts and using it every day, so we know what to do."

"Yay, Maria!" said Myrtle.

Judah raised his cane and said, "Sing it!"

Hide, hide, hide, I hide your Word in my heart.
Hide, hide, hide, I hide your Word in my heart.
So, I know what to do. So, I know what to do.
So, I know what to do, I won't sin against you.

Chapter 6

Walking on Water
(Matthew 14:22-33)

Do you ever make mistakes? We all do. Peter, one of Jesus' disciples, made a mistake while on an adventure with Jesus. Jesus did not get angry, he reached out and helped Peter. Join the ZP Running Club as they ride on Adam's duck boat and listen to Peter talk about his incredible adventure walking on the water with Jesus during a storm, on the Tale Spinner News Network. As Peter says, "This will be hard to believe, but it really happened to me."

"I wonder if all the kids have made it to the cove yet," asked Myrtle as she and Judah sat on their favorite bench in Zechariah Park.

"Maybe we should run over to the cove and join them," chuckled Judah.

"The only way I'm going to the cove is riding in Adam's duck boat," announced Myrtle.

Judah smiled. "Do you remember how the ZP Running Club started?"

Myrtle patted her heart. "I do. If Elle had not hidden God's Word in her heart and remembered that a friend always loves, she would not have been a good friend to Livi, and the running club might not have started."

"And now we have the ZP Running Club and an Annual Fun Run. The kids are excited about running from the Landing to the cove, sleeping in tents, and

running back to the Landing tomorrow. Good things happen when you hide God's Word in your heart," said Judah as he patted his heart.

Suddenly, over the sound of birds singing and children playing in the park, they could hear quacking.

"There's Adam," said Myrtle.

The bright yellow and orange duck boat pulled up in front of the bench as Adam yelled, "There are the coolest grandparents ever."

Judah gave him a thumbs up while Myrtle called out, "Hi, Sweetie. What are you doing?"

"I am headed across the lake to take dinner to the ZP Running Club at the cove. Want to ride along?"

Myrtle jumped up off the bench, laughing as she replied, "I just told your Pops that the only way I would go to the cove is to ride in your duck boat, and now here you are. Let's go!"

Adam let down the ramp and held on to Myrtle's hand as she got on. Judah danced up the ramp, excited to see how his friends were doing after their run to the cove. The quacks rang out as Adam blew the horn. The boat cruised across the land to the edge of the lake and bounced into the water. Laughing, Judah said, "That is always so much fun!"

"It will take a few minutes to get across the lake so sit back, take in the beautiful scenery and relax," encouraged Adam.

Myrtle closed her eyes and enjoyed the peacefulness of the lake as Judah watched a mama mallard and her eight baby ducks float across the water.

In the distance, the trees at the opening to the cove came into view. "We are almost there," Adam announced.

"We are excited to see our friends and hear about the run. I hope they had fun," said Myrtle.

Adam drove through the trees into the shallow waters of the cove then up onto the shore. He turned off the duck boat and blew the horn as the three visitors were greeted by hellos, hugs and high fives.

The parents helped Adam bring the food to the picnic tables as the kids gathered around. Livi's dad thanked God for the food, and everyone began eating and sharing stories about the day.

Once dinner was over, Elle's dad began building a fire and asked Myrtle, Judah and Adam if they would like to stay for the bonfire.

Adam replied that the duck boat did not have bright lights, so they needed to get back across the lake before dark.

"When you get to be an old man like me, you can ride across the lake instead of running around it," laughed Judah. "We will be waiting at the finish line for you tomorrow."

"Mr. Judah," said Elle with a twinkle in her eye, "Jesus wasn't old, and He didn't have to walk around the lake. He just walked across on top of the water."

Everyone laughed as Myrtle patted her heart and said, "Yay, Elle! You have hidden that Bible story in your heart."

"That gives me a great idea," said Adam. "How about once you cross the finish line tomorrow, I will have the duck boat loaded up with snacks, and you can all climb aboard. I will take you across the lake, the easy way, and we can watch the Tale Spinner News Network to see Jesus walk on the water. Anyone interested?"

Cheers rang out across the cove as the kids yelled, "Yes!"

"As Pops would say, coolio! Sleep well under the stars, and have a safe run back to the Landing," said Adam as he and his grandparents climbed onto the duck boat for the trip back across the lake.

The next day, the Zechariah Park families gathered at the Landing to cheer for the ZP Running Club as they returned from their adventure.

"Here they come!" cried Myrtle as she caught a glimpse of Johnny, Elle and Isaiah coming down the path. The runners seemed to slow down as they got close to the finish line. Everyone wondered what was going on but, before long, each member of the running

club patted their hearts, held hands and walked across the finish line together.

Judah and Myrtle yelled, "Yay, kids! You did it!" The ZP families cheered.

As Livi walked by Judah, he asked, "Hey, Livi, why did you all hold hands and walk across the finish line together?"

Livi smiled and began, "Last night, around the bonfire, Elle's dad was reading some important Bible verses to us. He said it would be great to be the first one across the finish line, but it is just as important to remember that the Bible tells us to be kind, love others as Jesus loves us and treat others as you want them to treat you.

"I remembered how hard it was for me when I first started running, and I would not have wanted to be the last one across the finish line. Since this was not an actual race but a fun adventure, I thought it might be the right thing to do to cross the finish line together. I have been working on hiding Philippians 4:5 in my heart, and it says, 'Let your gentleness be evident to all.' I thought instead of bragging about who finished first, we should do what the Bible says and let everyone see our kindness and gentleness to each other.

"Everyone liked my idea. Grace suggested we pat our hearts and hold hands as we walked across the line.

We thought that would be what Jesus would want us to do."

Myrtle patted her heart and said, "I am proud of you kids! Keep hiding God's Word in your heart. Adam is waiting for the running club at his duck boat. Have fun watching the Tale Spinner News Network about Jesus walking on the water."

The running club climbed on the duck boat, grabbed snacks and found a comfortable place to sit. They were tired after their run and happy to sit down with a snack to rest.

"Let's get out on the water before we pull out the Tale Spinner News Network. Hold on," cautioned Adam as the duck boat bounced down the pier and into the water. Once they were floating peacefully, Adam passed around a basket of Tale Spinner glasses. "Remember, you cannot see the story without these glasses. Are you ready?"

While putting on his own Tale Spinner glasses, Adam laughed just like his grandfather and said, "I love this part!" He pushed the button on the pocket of his belt, and the Tale Spinner flew out. When Adam lifted it to his mouth and blew, out popped the Tale Spinner News Network.

"It's showtime. Here we go!"

Hi, kids! I am Peter, one of Jesus' disciples. You may have heard about me before when everyone called me by my old name, Simon. One day, Jesus changed my name to Peter, which means "rock." Now everyone calls me Peter.

I have an incredible story about an adventure I had with Jesus. This will be hard to believe, but it really happened to me. Jesus became well known when He was living on Earth, and people followed Him everywhere. Jesus loved them all so much that He always took time to talk with them.

Jesus was God's Son, but when He lived on the earth, He was human too. That means He got tired, had to rest and needed to spend time praying to His Father in Heaven. We had been traveling and working hard. Jesus had just spent hours teaching and then performed a miracle to feed a large, hungry crowd using a little boy's lunch. After all of this, Jesus wanted to go up in the hills to pray. He told us to go to the other side of the lake where He would meet us later.

It was already dark and, as the boat headed out into the water, we hoped for a smooth ride so we could take turns sleeping. Bartholomew stayed awake to watch the weather. When the wind began to pick up, he knew a storm was brewing and we could be in trouble, so he woke us up. The winds kept getting stronger and the waves bigger. The boat began to rock back and forth as it started to rain. A loud clap of thunder crashed in the distance as James said, "We need to get ready for this storm."

The waves were crashing against the boat, and we were afraid we were going to sink and drown.

Bartholomew said, "I would feel so much better about being here if Jesus were with us."

Jesus knew we were in trouble and scared, so He decided to come to us.

Suddenly a streak of lightning crashed across the dark sky, and we saw something gliding toward us across the top of the water. Thomas was afraid it was a ghost.

Then we heard Jesus' voice, "Be courageous. It is me, Jesus. Don't be afraid."

I could not believe what I was seeing. Jesus was calmly walking towards us on top of the water even as thunder roared, lightning crashed, and waves rolled all around him. I had been around Jesus so much that I knew He could do anything, so I called out, "Jesus, if that is really You, let me walk on the water to You."

As a giant wave hit the boat, I heard Jesus say, "Come on, Peter."

I took a deep breath, gathered all my courage and stepped out of the boat. As my feet hit the water,

I was so nervous. I looked right at Him and kept taking steps. It was awesome. I was really walking on the water with Jesus!

Suddenly a big wave hit me, and lightning streaked across the sky. I looked away from Jesus and down at the roaring waves beneath my feet. I fell into the sea and screamed, "Jesus, help me!"

Jesus reached out and pulled me out of the water and put me back in the boat. Then He asked, "What happened, Peter? Why did you doubt?"

Jesus stepped into the boat and, immediately, the wind and rain stopped, and the sea became still.

Even the winds and the waves obeyed Jesus. No one else could do this. Jesus really was the Son of God.

Walking on the water with Jesus was a great adventure, and if I had kept looking at Him, everything would have been fine. That is just like your life. If you keep hiding God's Word in your heart and doing the right thing, Jesus will help you as you walk through each day. He did not get mad at me when I fell into the water, and He will not get mad at you when you mess up either. Ask Him to forgive you and help you do better. Then get back up and follow Him. He loves you.

As their Tale Spinner glasses went dark, Adam said, "That's a wrap," and hit the retract button on his belt. The Tale Spinner spun around and flew back into his belt's secret compartment.

Grace looked out at the water and said, "Peter must have been scared to get out of the boat. I would be scared if I had to get out and walk on this lake."

"When Jesus told Peter to walk to Him, Peter knew Jesus would keep him safe. We can trust Jesus to keep us safe, too," explained Adam as he patted Grace on the shoulder.

Adam looked over at Nori who was staring out at the lake and asked, "What are you thinking about, Nori?"

She smiled and said, "I think it is cool that Jesus wasn't angry when Peter took his eyes off Jesus and fell into the water."

"Me, too," agreed Carlos. "I liked when Peter told us Jesus did not get mad at him for messing up, and He won't get mad at us either."

Adam smiled as he told them, "The story of Jesus walking on the water is recorded in the Bible in three different places. That means it is important. Jesus wants us to always focus on Him, so we don't sink or fall or really mess up. When we do make mistakes, as everyone does, we should ask Jesus to forgive us, get up, dust ourselves off and try again."

"Try again. I will try running again tomorrow, but I'm tired today," said Maria. "I need to go home. Thank you, Adam, for the snacks, the duck boat ride and showing us the miracle of Jesus walking on the water."

Maria stood up and said to the others, "Let's do what Mr. Judah would do if he were here right now."

Isaiah yelled, "Sing it!"

Hide, hide, hide, I hide your Word in my heart.
Hide, hide, hide, I hide your Word in my heart.
So, I know what to do. So, I know what to do.
So, I know what to do, I won't sin against you.

Chapter 7
The End of Summer Bash

It is the last day of summer and Zechariah Park is celebrating with an End of Summer Bash. The families of ZP have spent the summer, at Adam's Landing, learning about some of the miracles Jesus performed while he lived on the earth. Hearing the stories from the Bible and then remembering the lessons they teach, is hiding God's Word in your heart. Let's join Judah and the ZP families as they begin the End of Summer Bash by singing, "Hide, Hide, Hide, I hide your Word in my heart...."

"...So, I know what to do, I won't sin against you."

"Well, that was fun," Judah said excitedly, as the ZP families finished the song and then broke into applause.

"Let's get this Marvelous Miracle Match competition started. My dear Myrtle designed activities to resemble each miracle we learned about this summer, and she is going to tell you about each one." Judah started to hand the microphone to his wife, then suddenly took it back to ask, "Isn't she beautiful?"

The ZP families loved Myrtle, and they gave her a giant cheer as she took the microphone and began speaking.

"Thanks, Sweet Judah. Hey, Zechariah Park. I had so much fun designing these activities for the Marvelous Miracle Match, and I hope you have fun doing them. Since we have five teams, there are five stations set up outside for each activity. The whole team must finish before your team can move on to the next activity.

Here they are in the order the teams will do them.

"First is the Water into Wine—You'll find large pots on the lake shore at station one. Take a bucket down to the lake, fill it with water, run back to the pot and dump the water into the pot. Pass the bucket to the next team member and continue getting water from the lake until the pot is full.

"Second is Fishers of Men—With your team, throw a fishing net into the little blow-up pool where plastic fish are floating. Once you have five fish in your net, gather the net and put it in the box by the pool. If you drop any of your fish, you must start over.

"Third is Calming the Storm—One person from each team must climb into the boat, grab the cushion and pretend to sleep on the seat while your team rocks the boat back and forth for 20 seconds.

"Next is Walking on the Water—You'll find five beams in the shallow part of the lake. Each team must walk across the beam in the lake without falling off. Anyone who falls off must start over.

"Last of all is Feeding the 5,000—Each team has an area with bread scattered on the ground. You must pick up all the leftover bread from the ground in your area and put it in your team's basket.

"We know that if you are hiding God's Word in your heart, you are already a winner—but the first team to finish all five activities and make it across the finish line wins this competition. Judah and I will be waiting at the finish line, ready to dance, sing and celebrate with you. Now, the best grandson in the world is here to give you last minute instructions. Here's Adam," Myrtle called out happily.

The ZP crowd began chanting, "Adam, Adam, Adam," as Myrtle handed over the microphone.

Adam kissed his grandmother on the cheek. "Thanks, Gran." Looking out over the crowd, he began, "Have you had fun this summer?"

"Yes!" The crowd roared.

"Coolio! The fun is not over yet. This Marvelous Miracle Match competition is going to be fun, too. Before we get started, how many of you visited the ZPH3 Theater to see The Tale Spinner News Network reports?"

Hands went up all through the crowd.

"Those miracles were amazing but remember that Jesus Himself is the greatest miracle. He loves you. He wants to be with you and help you in all you do. All you have to do is ask Him. Now, let's get this Marvelous Miracle Match started.

Teams, you have three minutes to go outside and get in place at the starting line. I will meet you there," instructed Adam as he started his stopwatch.

The teams ran outside and the ZP families followed.

Adam walked over to the starting line as his stopwatch beeped. "It looks like you all are ready. Have fun, and we will see you at the finish line!"

He called out to the crowd, "Count down with me."

The ZP residents began, "10, 9, 8, 7, 6, 5, 4, 3, 2, 1."

"Go!" yelled Adam.

Acting out the miracles of Jesus they learned about over the summer was fun and a lot of laughter could be heard in Zechariah Park. Livi and Carlos knocked over the water pot at the first station and had to start over. Ava stepped on the net and ripped it, so her fish

kept falling out. Rosie was laughing so hard she could not pretend to sleep in the boat for 20 seconds. Isaiah had to start over walking on the beam in the water because he was making sounds like the wind and thunder and lost his balance, several times. Miles and Maria picked up all the bread on the ground quickly, but they put it in the wrong basket; so, they had to start over, too.

Finally, the first team crossed the finish line, and Myrtle and Judah began dancing, just as they had promised. It did not take long for the other teams to follow.

Adam took the mic and announced, "Congratulations to Nori, Elle, Grace, Lucas and Johnny for winning! They are ZP's Magnificent Miracle Match Champions. Give them a hand."

The ZP families cheered for their friends.

Adam high-fived the winners as he repeated, "Congrats again, guys! Remember what my Gran said before we began. Everyone who hides God's Word in their heart by hearing the stories in the Bible and remembering them is a winner. Just like some of Jesus' disciples shared their stories with us on the Tale Spinner News Network, we can share Jesus with our friends and family by how we act and what we say. We should try our best every day to follow Jesus and keep hiding His Word in our hearts. Let's be fishers of men wherever we go.

"Thanks for coming to Adam's Landing this summer. I'm looking forward to many more fun times together. Have a . . ."

"Wait!" yelled Judah. "We can't end this fun day without singing our favorite song one more time."

Judah raised his cane and called out, "Sing it!"

Hide, hide, hide, I hide your Word in my heart.
Hide, hide, hide, I hide your Word in my heart.
So, I know what to do. So, I know what to do.
So, I know what to do, I won't sin against you.

Thanks for reading
Zechariah Park: Adam's Landing!

If you enjoyed reading it,
please consider leaving a review on
Amazon.com and anywhere else that
accepts book reviews. Your review will
help new readers discover Myrtle and
Judah and perhaps we can all hide God's
Word in our hearts together!

Check out
cindyholtmiller.com
to keep up with Myrtle and Judah
and learn about their upcoming
adventures!

About the Author

Cindy Holt Miller is a mother and grandmother who has enjoyed making up tales since she was a little girl and now, as an author, she gets to share those tales, with children of all ages everywhere.

After spending thirty years as an elementary school teacher and administrator, she has a heart for sharing Biblical principles, in a fun and easily relatable way with the next generation.

Cindy lives in Central Indiana but enjoys escaping to a sunny beach whenever possible.

About the Illustrator

Joe Eckstein is the illustrator of over twenty-five books for children, including *Herby Gets a Life*, which he also authored. Drawing and writing stories since he can remember, he grew up in central Ohio, holds a Bachelor's degree in Fine Art, and has worked as a staff illustrator for a leading children's educational publisher as well as an art and theatre teacher at a Christian school.

Joe lives in Florida and is devoted to the wife of his youth, Kristen. In addition to creating art, he enjoys singing, dancing, performing theatre, traveling, being outdoors, and spending time with family. Learn more about Joe and his work at www.JoeEckstein.com.

CPSIA information can be obtained
at www.ICGtesting.com
Printed in the USA
BVHW041158080622
639117BV00012B/417